beautiful, NOT BROKEN

A JOURNEY OF SELF-LOVE

KRYSTLE A. BARRINGTON

Beautiful, Not Broken: A Journey of Self-Love

Copyright © 2024 by Krystle A. Barrington
Chasing Butterflies Publishing

Second Edition

Paperback ISBN: 978-0-9967085-6-2
eBook ISBN: 978-0-9967085-7-9

All poems, quotes, and prayers are original works by the author. All rights reserved. This book or any portion thereof may not be reproduced or used in any manner whatsoever without the express written permission of the publisher. Manufactured in the United States of America.

Edited by Val Pugh Love
Cover and Book Design by Kristy Twellmann Hill • umbrellasquared.com
Cover Photo by Vie Studio • Pexels.com

For every girl figuring out who she is and every woman who has found herself through pain.

INTRO

When I first came up with the idea to write this book, it scared me a little bit. I was afraid because it meant sharing parts of myself that weren't so pretty, polished, or put together. My truth is that for most of my life, I have struggled with my self-esteem. It took me a very long time to begin feeling comfortable in my own skin. As a result of not feeling good enough, I sought after all the wrong things. My poison of choice was connecting my body, my time, and my energy to relationships that only hindered my personal growth. Frankly, I was lost, desperate for validation, and willing to give parts of myself to feel special—even if it was temporary. I've discovered that people or things can't make us whole or fix us. Only God can do that.

As I entered my thirties, I decided that I needed to make some serious changes in how I was moving through life. That meant taking a very hard look at my choices, my personal issues, and most importantly, my relationship with Christ. As this shift continues to happen in my life, it hasn't been all hearts and unicorns. Sometimes my mind still goes wild. Sometimes my thoughts are just not the right thoughts. Sometimes I find myself wanting to shrink back from everyone and everything. That's my truth, and I own it.

In these pages, I've shared pieces of this journey with you. It is the pursuit of self-love in all its glory. From dark moments to beautiful reminders, this is my story. It is a journey of learning to see myself as God sees me so that I never feel like I have to settle in any area of my life. I hope that the words you read in this book will be a source of encouragement to you in some way. More importantly, I hope it triggers you to look deeper at the way you see yourself and how self-love influences your decisions and quality of life.

REDEEMED *love*

I used to lay down next to rejection.
I sold my soul to the devil for fleeting moments of affection.
I fell in love with the idea of love,
while dismissing the greatest love I've ever known.
And the further my heart drifted from God,
the more desperate I became for validation.
I was lost.
I was broken.
Yet, God's love was always there…
Always hovering over me in the best way possible…
Never leaving my side.
And even as I lay next to loneliness,
He saw fit to reach down and save my soul.
He breathed life into my heart again.
He saved me in more ways than one.
And now I live for Him.
I breathe for Him.
I give my life to Him because He loves me.
He loved me when I didn't love myself.
And while man rejected me,
He kept me.
Always.

The love of God is something that we often take for granted. Just imagine Christ sent His darling son Jesus Christ to die for the sins He knew we would commit. And even now, He loves us past our sins, our struggles, our demons, and even our secrets. His Love is true. It is constant. It is golden. It is the only love worth chasing.

HELLO *beautiful*

You are my daughter.
And even if you cannot see it just yet,
I want to tell you how beautiful you are.
See, I loved you before you were conceived.
I believed in you before you ever believed in yourself.
Those rough edges you have are not imperfections at all.
They are merely your beauty marks.
Those scars you wish you could erase so quickly
should not trigger shame,
but rather put a flame under your strength.
Your beauty is far greater than labels or *likes*.
Your purpose is rooted in Me and Me alone.
You are loved.
You are my child.
You are beautiful simply because I say so.

— God

Falling in love is so much easier than falling out of it. I wish it wasn't so. I stayed when I should have left. The writings were on the wall, but I couldn't help myself. I gave too much of myself physically, mentally, and emotionally. Now, I'm looking around in a daze wishing I could get that time back. I'm looking in the mirror confused because I set myself up for heartbreak. I could beat myself up about it. I could walk around in shame. But, rather than waste more energy on things I cannot change, I must look ahead. I must learn from my mistakes. I've got to do what I've got to do so I never have to stare the same hurt in the face ever again.

CARDIAC *arrest*

I loved him the best way I knew how at the time.
The truth is, I was as broken as ever.
Then the cracks began to spread,
and when it reached the heart, it only triggered more pain,
confusion, and self-destruction.
My heart couldn't take it anymore.
It stopped beating for all the things that gave it life -
The good things like joy and peace.
Instead, lust crept in like a thief in the night.
Doubt followed me around on both shoulders.
I was tired.
My heart could no longer survive such pressure,
and now I realize that I could not love another until I learned to love myself.

Society tells me I should be married already. Society tells me that I am somehow damaged goods because I'm over the age of thirty and don't have a ring on my finger. See, society doesn't know my story. Society hasn't wiped my tears when I felt heartbreak. Society didn't comfort me when I put myself out there. Society won't tell me that God's plans are better than my own. Society won't encourage me to wait for those plans to unfold. Society is impatient. Society is on a timetable. I refuse to let society tell me where I'm supposed to be at any given time. Society doesn't get to dictate my self-worth. Not today. Not tomorrow. Not ever.

BALANCE

A relationship should never become a band-aid.
It should never serve as a distraction to our deepest issues.
There must be a balance between growth and love.
In a perfect world, they both exist simultaneously,
Somewhere on Cloud 9 between pure bliss and self-love.
That's the kind of love I want...
The kind that doesn't suck the life out of me.
The kind that pushes me towards my truest potential.
I never want to choose again,
and I won't.

She decided to love herself unapologetically.
She decided **she** was the prize.
Set apart, more than her past,
and filled with so much promise.

UNRAVELED

Darkness is all around me.
The quietness is so loud that it frightens me.
With tears streaming down my face,
honesty is sitting in front of me.
I try to stand to my feet to run, but it pulls me back down.
I cannot escape this moment.
I've been running too long.
There are memories running through my mind.
Honesty tells me it's time to find healing.
It tells me that there is freedom in accepting my truth.
And so, I sit in my mess.
I think of the good, the bad, and the very ugly.
The ugly makes me cringe.
This is the beginning of freedom.
And as I begin to unravel my truth,
my heart begins to feel free.
Freedom from my own bondage…
Freedom to live…
Freedom to love…
Freedom to thrive…
Freedom from the heaviness of the past…

YOU ARE LOVED

Dear Younger Self,

Believe in yourself.
Believe in the power that lives inside you.
Believe in the scriptures you read.
Believe in your future enough to go for it.
Don't drag your feet, and never walk with
your head held down.
Be bold.
Be adventurous.
Don't stress over trivial things.
Don't place your value on what hangs in your closet.
Don't be timid.
Don't be afraid to mess up.
Take life by the reigns and live out loud!

P.S. I love you.

RISE

Rise, my sister.
You are a gem.
You were created to walk in the light.
You are a light.
I see your essence.
I recognize your power.
Made in His image.
Created for greatness.
Beautiful in every sense of the word.
Understand you have a purpose.
You deserve the absolute best.
Stand tall.
Stand bold.
Rise, my sister.

Don't settle for being a secret or an afterthought. You are worth a title. You are worthy of respect and honesty, even in your absence.

GOD IS *love*

There is something about falling in love with Jesus.
It's a journey like no other.
He will reach down to the deepest part of our souls
and speak to us in a way that no one else can.
It's as if the Holy Spirit speaks its own language -
A language that is unique to each of us.
And the voice of God covers us from head to toe.
In His arms, we are safe.
In His presence, we are protected.
His love is magnificent to the highest power.
It's infectious.
It's so overpowering.
The deepest affection we will ever experience.
He is love.

Your life is not your own. It belongs to God. And anything that belongs to God has VICTORY written all over it. So, stop focusing on all the things not going right in your life, and embrace the journey. Your breakthrough won't come when everything is perfect in your life. It will come when you decide to see past your troubles while you're still in it.

CROWNS

He moved on,
and she looks nothing like me.
From her frame to her skin tone,
she is everything I am not.
It is not her beauty that bothers me.
It is the idea that I was never what he wanted.
It is the notion that I was just a void filler -
Convenience at its best.
I could drive myself crazy with speculation.
I could let comparison get the best of me.
Instead, I'll just adjust my crown and walk away,
because deep down I always knew it wasn't meant to be.

Lord,

Take me higher in my faith, my discipline, my creativity, and my drive. I pray that every trial will only boost my faith and that every setback will put a fire in me. Thank you for choosing me. Thank you for calling me your daughter and equipping me with all I need. For your glory, I live. For your glory, I will pursue my purpose.

Amen.

danger ZONE

To lust is our flesh seeking temporary gratification.
To love is to seek something deeper than physical touch.
Love can make you throw out all logic.
Lust will distract us from our purpose.
Guard your heart and protect your mind, my friend, because both can be dangerous in their own way.

Never love someone so hard that you become soft at protecting your very own soul.

MOVING ON

Moving on from the past isn't easy.
Forgetting the one you love is no small feat.
And when you're in the thick of it,
it might feel like you will never be free…
Free from the memories that feel like shadows…
Free from the what-ifs that only drive you crazy…
Free from the moments when your imagination goes wild.
Things might be hard, but the memories will soon fade.
Take the time to tend to your wounds.
Take things one day at a time,
and hold on to every ounce of peace you get back.

Distance doesn't cure a broken heart. It will follow you around wherever you go until you decide to acknowledge your hurt, your role, and your strength to move on with no regrets.

wait FOR IT...

Some people pray for forever.
I pray that I won't miss God's blessings.
I hope that my heart will be open
to what God has for me.
And if that be love, I trust that it will come when He sees fit.
I'm not interested in quieting the spectators who so desire for
me to be in a relationship.
I'm more concerned with positioning myself to be ready for
all God has for me—
His plans, not mine.

Self-reflection is merely the ability to have a growing relationship with ourselves. Don't get comfortable with denial. Instead, be courageous enough to examine yourself and your decisions in an effort to live better and do better.

MIRACLES OF *love*

I've become the single girl in the group.
No ring on my finger, I am now the minority.
And while friendships change and priorities shift,
I focus on standing boldly in the season I am in.
No time for tears or worry.
I'm going to focus on being the best version of myself.
And when the time is right,
my forever will be a beautiful surprise,
an answered prayer,
and a miracle of sorts.

Her insecurities no longer hold her captive because she has realized perfection doesn't exist. She began to place her value in the hands of God. She decided to show herself grace along the way. Her decision to love herself beyond the judgment of others or the false idea that she wasn't good enough saved her. And now, she lives her life knowing that her potential is more significant than any mistake she ever made.

the PREPARATION

I'd like to think that I haven't
seen my best day yet.
It seems like the more I experience life,
the more I understand that God is on a mission
to blow my mind.
I don't always like when He is pruning me,
but it comforts me to know that
He is just preparing me for more.

Comparison will steal your joy, break your confidence, and transform boldness into fear. Remember that you were not created to be anyone but yourself. God has not called you to be like anyone else in this world. Use your energy to be you and only you.

HIGHER

'Round and 'round we go,
living in insanity,
expecting different results.
It's time to wake up.
Live intentionally.
Let your light shine in a world
that so desperately needs good.
A lot of good…
Be an inspiration.
And live your life going in one direction—
Higher.

There is no such thing as "relationship goals" when you don't know what a relationship is battling behind closed doors. Don't worship the illusion that perfect relationships exist, because they don't. Admire maybe, but understand that you may not be built for the very relationship you worship.

LETTING *go*

And when she forgave,
the sun began to shine.
She found clarity once more,
and her heart began tc beat again.

NO TIME FOR
TEARS OR WORRY

Sometimes I feel like my life is missing something, and more often than not, that something is resting in God's presence. Life gets so busy that it can be exhausting and distracting. We should always remember that God's word is meant to lift us up every day. Without it, we will eventually fall to our knees in desperation.

THE END OF A *season*

And even though things didn't work out,
it doesn't mean it wasn't real for me.
You were a lesson I had to learn,
and the experience was not in vain.
I choose to grow from this experience.
I choose to see it as a season
that has now come to an end.

When we stop making decisions out of moments of loneliness, impatience, and fickle emotions, that's when we truly begin to understand that God's best for our lives has absolutely nothing to do with us. God isn't logical. He is spiritual, and everything He does has a purpose in it.

DECISIONS

We all fail God sometimes.
We all mess up.
We can choose pity,
or we can choose change.
We can blame the world,
or we can take responsibility.
We can choose denial,
or we can choose to rise above.
We can shrink back,
or we can bounce back.
The choice is ours.

Loyalty should never be confused with setting yourself back in an effort to not disappoint someone else. So, don't go broke trying to help someone. Don't sabotage your own joy to help someone. Don't ignore the calling on your life to entertain a relationship that has no substance. Simply put, anybody who truly values you would never ask you to compromise yourself to help them.

TRUE *love*

Love hasn't been nice to me.
It has overpowered me...
Fooled me...
Mesmerized me...
It has wrecked me in the worst way,
but I haven't lost hope that true love exists.
I just know that if God is not rooted in it, I don't want it.
If it doesn't bring glory to God, I want no part of it.
I'm not waiting for butterflies.
Instead, I pray for purpose.
I'm no longer leaning on my own understanding.
I've decided that true love is on the other side of hearing God's voice.

Sometimes you have to look in the mirror and literally open your mouth and speak to yourself. Look at yourself in the mirror and remind yourself that you are everything God says you are. Forget what people have said or what they may be whispering about. Pick your self-esteem up off the floor and be the woman you were called to be. Seize the moment and stop talking yourself out of opportunities. You were not created to fail no matter what anyone has ever told you!

BLURRED *vision*

Smoking mirrors,
Blurred vision,
The pursuit of affection gone wrong…
Wipe your eyes.
Bid farewell to denial.
Accept hard truths.
No more self-sabotage…
No more self-destruction…
Choose freedom.
Choose truth.
Choose growth.

Every season has its own unique purpose, and in that season we must learn the intended lessons. But so often we miss them because we are in such a rush to get to the next chapter. I can tell you that turning pages is critical in life, but when we are rushed by emotion or selfish desires rather than the Holy Spirit, we stunt our growth. We're moving through life so fast that we often miss what God is trying to tell us. So, I urge you to slow down. I encourage you to soak it in. I beg you to see the beauty in where you are.

THE WAY HE *sees me*

Brown girl,
Beautiful girl,
Kissed with Melanin,
You are captivating,
Filled with magic,
Handpicked by God,
Designed in His image,
Created to bring Him glory,
Living in pursuit of joy,
Humbled by His Mercy,
Destined for greatness.
You are everything He says you are.

I'd like to think that walking with God is a journey and not a race. It is indeed a miraculous voyage characterized by peaks and valleys. There will be tears coupled with joy. There will be days filled with questions and days we are overwhelmed by His presence. And while we may not always get what we want, there is something about knowing that serving Him only leads to victory. There is power in knowing that our pain will never be in vain and God's hands are always covering us.

SEARCHING

She's beautiful on the outside,
empty on the inside.
Always searching for something,
yet that something can never be found
in anything on this earth.
With a chip on her shoulder,
she stumbles through life lost, angry, and dissatisfied.
Yearning for something deeper,
she struggles to put a finger on it.
Time passes her by.
Material things and superficial relationships can no longer
hold her head up.
Life becomes too heavy a burden to bear,
and then she has an epiphany.
Her identity must be rooted in something constant,
something greater than anything the world can give.
It is time to find her way back to her Father in heaven,
to the one whose love runs deep.
It is time to run back into the arms of her first love.

We can spend a lifetime falling for others but never truly love who we are.

YOU

You are enough,
with your flaws,
and despite your past.
You are chosen.
You are redeemed.
You are favored.
You are special.
You are enough.
You were created
to be who you are,
and not an imitation
of anyone else.

Figure out what makes you happy. I'm not talking about material things or companionship. I'm talking about those key elements of your life that truly make you feel good on the inside. Whether it be financially, spiritually, or physically, or a combination of all those things, give it your all! Do it for yourself, and don't apologize for it.

I CHOOSE

I choose growth.
I choose transparency.
I choose self-love.
I choose freedom from the past.
I choose to walk in redemption.
I choose joy.
I choose to smile.
I choose life.
I choose forgiveness.
I choose kindness.
I choose humility.
I choose victory.
I choose change.
I choose relationship over religion.
I choose God.

Hearing is not enough. Believing is not enough. Trusting in it and living by it is what will catapult us spiritually.

I AM

I am more than a single woman.
I am ambitious.
I am strong.
I am an overcomer.
I am a dreamer and a doer.
So, don't pity me.
Don't assume I'd like to trade places with the woman whose left hand is adorned by a ring.
Don't put me down.
Don't turn your nose up at me.
Help me celebrate where I am in this very moment.
Wish me well.
Pray for me.
Believe in me.
Understand that I am right where I need to be.

If your progression scares him, intimidates him, or doesn't motivate him, you just might need to let it go.

FREEDOM IN *forgiveness*

Forgiveness is personal freedom from hurt.
It is the conscious decision to let go at the
alter what we cannot change.
It is taking the blinders off and facing our hurt.
It is one of the most liberating feelings we
will ever experience.
But, it can also be painful and downright difficult.
It is a necessity if we want to move forward.
It can become baggage too heavy to bear.
Remember that forgiveness is for you,
your future, and your heart.

YOU ARE ENOUGH

Being comfortable in your own skin has nothing to do with other people. It has everything to do with the limits you choose to put on yourself. Your identity is greater than a number on a scale or the number of followers you have on social media. Remember, self-love is an inside job.

LORD, I thank you

I thank you for being a comforter.
I thank you for loving me when
I did not love myself.
I thank you for your grace.
I thank you for using me even in my mess.
I pray that I will be the woman
you have called me to be.
I hope that when I drift away,
your love would find me where I am and
speak to me like only you can.

Amen.

I didn't begin walking in my purpose until I walked away from dead relationships and started running towards God. My journey hasn't been perfect, and I think that's okay. With time, my perspective on life began to change and my joy became fixed on God, not man. I found my way back to my heavenly Father, and my life has changed for the better.

FLAWLESS

And while I'd love to be flawless,
I understand I am not.
I am a beautiful mess,
a complicated riddle,
an imperfect vessel,
filled with purpose and passion.

We should never walk away from a relationship and not take responsibility for our role. Taking a hard look in the mirror doesn't dismiss what the other person did but instead creates room for personal growth. We must be willing to acknowledge our ugly truths to turn them into lessons.

PERSPECTIVE

Standing still,
taking it all in,
realizing how blessed I truly am,
the good outshines the bad.
Completely wrecked by His favor,
life is good my friend.
I'm not waiting for all the pieces to fall into place.
I can no longer be anxious about the unknown.
Here, in this moment,
on this beautiful day,
I am basking in the now, the present, my current reality.
I am staring at contentment,
and it is a beautiful thing.

In the hustle and bustle of life, don't forget to celebrate yourself. Get dressed up. Raise your glass. Cheers to success, growth, and revelation. And, if you struggle to find something to celebrate, think about where you could be compared to where you are. Remember, there is nothing too small to celebrate.

PIECES OF *me*

One day I looked up,
and pieces of myself were no longer with me.
I took a look in the mirror,
almost scanning my body,
and it hit me.
Soul ties had robbed me.
I was so far from the presence
of God that it should have crushed me.
I felt used up in the worst way,
but on one glorious day, God spoke to me.
He told me how much He loved me.
He told me that my shortcomings didn't define me.
He reminded me that in Him I could
pick myself up.
He wrapped His arms around me and reminded
me that nothing could separate me from His love,
not even my indiscretions or selfish moments.
He saved me, again.

Life truly goes on when a relationship comes to an end. Don't let past hurts paralyze you while the other person is living life to the fullest, without a care in the world for what's going on in your life.

CROSSROADS

Let me tell you a story of a girl
who came to a crossroads.
Standing before her was a fork in the road.
To her left was self-destruction
and to her right was redemption.
To her left was a life full of sin,
and to her right was righteousness.
She stood there confused and a bit perplexed.
This would be a defining moment, and with a quiet prayer and
a deep breath, she began to run.
She ran as fast as she could, and with each step
she felt the presence of God.
She understood the road would be hard.
She understood she would be tempted.
She knew it wouldn't be easy,
but she also knew it would be worth it.

Imagine what would happen if we decided to put God in His rightful place in our lives. Imagine the joy we would experience. Imagine the peace we would have when life takes the wrong turn. Imagine what could happen if we decided to welcome God into every area of our lives. Just think about it.

FAITH IN *motion*

Life has taught me that this world can be brutal.
Faith has taught me that there is power in my prayers.
We were created to be victors, not victims.
So when life gets hard, let us find that place
where we remember who is truly in control.
Let us remember to be resilient and strong.
Let's remember to exercise our faith.

I've learned to not let unsolicited comments or relationship advice make me feel inadequate.
But, the older I get, the more I realize that society has made marriage a goal. It is a rite of passage of some sort, and if you don't experience it by a certain age, you are doomed, damaged, or a disappointment. Having struggled with my identity for far too long, I've decided to only be influenced by God's word and not the whispers of others. My identity is far greater than my relationship status.

SPEAK *life*

Your words have power,
so speak life.
Speak victory.
Speak faith.
Speak peace.
Speak joy.
Speak with authority.
Let your words be a positive force in your life.

I've discovered that it is only through God that we can experience real breakthroughs in our lives. We alone are not strong enough, but oh when we link arms with God's word, powerful things happen. I'm grateful that even in our mess He still cares for us, but when we give our hearts, our minds, and our lives to Jesus Christ in a new way, He will blow our minds away.

REFLECTIONS

There was a time when I lacked confidence.
I wondered if my skin was too dark,
or if my frame was too thin.
Deep down I felt like I wasn't good enough.
And so, I talked myself out of opportunities.
I sat in the back of the room hoping to not be seen or heard.
I pursued relationships that were dead from the beginning.
I failed to give myself a fighting chance to be all that I could be.
But then, I saw the light,
and the words I read in God's great book
began to jump off the pages and speak to me.
It literally brought me back to life.
And so now I live, not just for me, but for Him.
I gave my life back to Him.
I am grateful for His love, His mercy, and His grace.

We can chase the things of this world for a lifetime and never truly feel complete. Instead, let's chase God. Let's chase doing more good. Let's chase continued growth, healthy relationships, and self-love.

BUT GOD

No one has it all together.
No one lives a perfect life.
We all have a story,
and while we are all perfectly imperfect,
we are still chosen.
We are still beautiful.
We are still capable.
We are still strong.
We are not our past.
We are not our mistakes.
We are called to do amazing things.
Remember that you are worthy.
Remember that you haven't seen your best day yet.
Remember to give yourself some love along the way.
Remember to never chase perfection.

Hurt and brokenness have the power to change who we are. They can silently turn us into our own worst enemy by transforming our thoughts, our actions, and even our attitudes in the most negative way. Therefore, it is our responsibility to guard our hearts, to turn them inside out and examine ourselves daily, to sit face-to-face with our truth, and to love ourselves enough to evolve.

REDEFINING BEAUTY

A pretty face is just a pretty face,
but a woman filled with kindness,
a woman who shows humility,
a woman who is willing to reach back
and help someone,
a woman who thrives off of positivity,
a woman who encourages others,
a woman who is honest,
a woman whose heart seeks God daily,
that is beauty.

YOUR WORDS HAVE POWER

It's never a good feeling when we experience hurt of any kind. What's more tragic is allowing it and indirectly encouraging it. Every relationship or friendship we have must have boundaries and mutual respect. Without that, it won't last.

SWEET *silence*

We tend to get restless when things are quiet.
When we are praying for things and nothing is happening around us, we tend to get a little anxious.
The funny thing is that God is always working on our behalf, and even if we don't see it at this very moment, God is not quiet.
Don't be freaked out, my friend.
Trust the process.
Trust His timing.
Trust that He has your back a million times over.

Stop waiting for someone to tell you how amazing you are when you have every right to tell yourself.

AUTHENTICITY

Be who you were created to be.
Some will like you and some won't.
Some will support you and some won't.
Stay in your lane and focus your energy on
being who you were called to be.
The rest will fall in place.

Fear is nothing but the devil trying to suffocate the calling over your life. In those moments when you feel like your goals are impossible, cry out to God. Ask God for confidence. Ask Him for direction. Ask Him to make a way for you. Ask Him to give you the confidence you need to rise to the occasion. I promise you, He will answer your every prayer.

FALLING

She was falling,
and in the midst of losing focus,
she began to question her place on this earth.
Overcome by insecurities,
she fell further and further away from her purpose.
And so it became more and more difficult
to find her way.
And so, she grabbed hold of anything and anyone she could.
But then, God gave her a glimpse of what life could be;
A life full of surrendering all things to Him.
And once her feet were planted on solid ground,
that is when her eyes were opened;
that is when she began to fall for God.

You didn't come this far to go back. Whether it be a relationship that never had God's approval, feelings of loneliness, lack of confidence, or even self-doubt, don't go back. Don't turn back the hands of time due to temporary emotions. Don't let momentary emotions push you back into a place you worked so hard to rise above. Dig deep and never look back!

THIS *walk*

This walk isn't meant to be easy.
It is meant to stretch and pull and tease our faith,
to exercise our patience,
to quiet our selfish desires in hopes of bringing God glory.
It requires sacrifice like no other.
It is demanding, and our God is jealous.
It will bring tears to our eyes.
It will push us to throw out all logic
and put our trust in our Father,
turning our eyes from what is seen
and holding on to what is unseen.
But we are not in this alone.
We are surrounded by something greater,
something bigger than any problem.
May life push us towards Him and not away.
May we learn to hold hands with Jesus.
Let us not be ashamed of where He brought us
and embrace where He is taking us.
Let us walk with God.

Time will not wait for you to overcome your fears. It will pass right by you, and one day you'll wonder what exactly you did with yourself over the years. You will look around and realize that for most of your life, you fell in that category of a dreamer and not a doer. You will feel a sense of panic as it sinks in that it literally is now or never. Just go for it. Throw your fears to the wind, and let your faith guide you. Let the story of your life finally unfold, and take God along with you.

SOLO

She decided to give her life back to Christ,
and before her eyes, she lost friends.
She no longer got invites she used to receive,
and she was no longer considered a good time.
But, on a brighter note, she gained clarity.
She gained perspective.
She said goodbye to anxieties.
She began to trust in God.
She may have lost a few people along the way,
but she gained peace, strength, and purpose
in the process.

A people created to be set apart will never fit in with a world that promotes everything but God. Stop trying to fit in, and stop waiting for everyone to like you. God will send who you need and what you need at the appointed time. You just need to believe in yourself enough to go for it, and let God do the rest.

GOING *up*

I want to prosper in every area of my life -
To be financially stable,
To be physically fit,
To be emotionally responsible,
To be mentally sound,
To learn something new about God daily...
Every day on a steady incline.

The hardest part about learning to love myself was accepting the fact that I could not rewind time and right some wrongs. I had to learn to show myself some grace. Once I finally understood that my past was my past, that is when I started to change my perspective about who I was and who I wanted to be. I had to remove the distractions. I had to walk away from people I still cared about. I had to start being intentional about respecting myself.

the STRUGGLE

We want it to be easy.
We want our prayers answered immediately.
We want life to be a walk in the park.
We want things quick and fast,
but that's not reality.
And, without tough times,
our faith will never be stretched,
our perspectives will never evolve,
and we would never truly understand
the power that lives inside of us.

We make decisions every single day, all in the name of loving other people. Watch what happens when you start to make decisions all in the name of better loving yourself. Don't confuse this with being self-centered. This is about being conscious about where we put ourselves on our very own priority list. This has everything to do with being intentional about breaking cycles, owning our healing process, and taking charge of our mental and emotional state.

do IT

Don't let life swallow you whole.

Don't let your sorrows hold you at night.

Be careful not to let your anxieties steal your joy.

Live, my sister.

Feel the sun on your face.

Sit quietly and listen to the rain.

Be still in the darkness.

You are alive.

Life is full of opportunities.

You have work to do,

so get up.

Dream big.

Talk yourself into pursuing your dreams.

Live and laugh and sing and twirl and dance and write.

Whatever you fancy, do it.

I would have experienced a lot less hurt in my life had I not been stubborn about wanting who and what I wanted when I wanted it. At the end of the day, if we truly want God's best for our lives, we've got to surrender. As long as we are filled with sin, we don't have all the answers. The minute we decide we have it all figured out, we set ourselves up for more heartbreak.

DEAR *destiny,*

I'm coming for you.
I ran from you for way too long.
I always knew greater days were ahead,
but I wasn't strong enough to fight for it.
My focus was off,
and frankly, I didn't truly want it.
But today, I believe in myself like never before.
Success, I see you,
and there's no talking me out of it.
This time, I'm giving it my all.
There will be setbacks,
but my life wasn't designed for failure.

Yours Truly,
An Overcomer

It doesn't matter how much of yourself you give, either someone cherishes you or they don't. Hear me; people will suck you dry for everything you have if you let them, so pay attention. Don't be so desperate for affection that your imagination gets the best of you. Remember, the truth will always set us free. Always.

S.O.S.

If He hadn't come to rescue me,
I'd still be completely lost.
I'd still be searching for that something.
I wouldn't know that I am indeed of value.
I would still be holding on to false hope.
I'd still be focused on looking put together.
I'm grateful that He rescued me from my own thoughts.
At my lowest point of distress,
He heard my cries.
The journey could have killed me.
It could have killed my spirit.
Oh, but God.

TOUGH TIMES STRETCH OUR FAITH

Who we are as women is largely influenced by how we deal with our baggage, and yes, we all have it. While we don't always get to choose our baggage, we do have a responsibility to ourselves to examine that baggage and not run from it. It's not always pretty, but your baggage doesn't have to have power over you. And, if it does, take that power back.

OLDER AND *wiser*

They say that your twenties are
the years you lose yourself.
Your thirties are the years you find yourself.
I'm not sure what the forties and on
are supposed to be about,
but I can tell you that with each decade,
I hope I become better.
I hope I learn to live better
and go harder for what I want.
Most importantly, I hope to discover more about God.
I hope I never revisit past hurts.
I pray I don't regress,
but rather continue to show progress.
I hope to God that I become a woman
that He is proud of.

Stop waiting for an apology you will never get. Stop waiting for someone to acknowledge your pain. We can't send someone the message that it's okay to treat us like an option, and then cry when we aren't a priority. I stretched myself thin time and time again, and for not much in return. That's how little I felt about myself. I didn't appreciate what I brought to the table enough to demand respect. *Don't make that mistake.*

TO BE *content*

I've decided to protect my heart.
I've seen too much.
I've endured too much.
So, I pray for discernment.
I pray for strength.
I'm looking forward and not behind me.
I guard my heart at all costs.
I am learning to sit in God's presence;
So content that I'm not worried about the future
but enjoying the beauty of the present.

And, when we decide to truly start walking with God daily, the things that used to consume our thoughts will drift away, and the strongholds that kept us captive will break loose. It may not happen overnight, but with continued prayer and discipline, it can happen.

I CHOOSE *you*

As I continue to go through life, I will choose you.
I will love you hard and unapologetically.
I will take care of you.
I will not turn a blind eye to when you're hurting.
I will speak life over you.
I will choose you when others do not.
I will pray for you.
I will pick you up when you fall.
I will make you a priority.
I will respect you.
I will read God's word.
I will trust God's promises.
I will set you up high like the queen that you are.
I will love you past your mistakes.
I will examine you.
I will choose you.
I will choose me.

Lord,

Help me to control my thoughts. Give me the ability to redirect my thoughts when they wander too far from your word. Help me to catch myself when I become too critical of my choices. Remind me that I am yours even when life causes me to doubt. Thank you for uplifting me when I need it the most.

Amen.

NOTE FROM THE *author*

Hello Sister,

I hope that this glimpse of my own struggles with finding myself has blessed you in some way. More importantly, I hope it sparks something deep down inside of you. What you feel when you look in the mirror is powerful. It has the power to lift you up or push you in a corner. When we are not comfortable with who we are, it will manifest itself in other areas of our lives. It won't look the same for all of us, but ultimately, I truly believe that the only way to conquer those negative feelings is to begin seeing ourselves the way God sees us.

Our ability to dig deep and not hide from issues is hard, but it is so freeing. Therefore, as you move through life, I challenge you to own your mistakes and take pride in the fact that you survived. Don't let poor choices or seasons of recklessness make you feel like you aren't good enough, because that is a complete lie. You are everything God says you are. It doesn't matter what you've done, where you've been, or who you did it with, through God's eyes, you are beautiful, not broken.

Krystle

ABOUT THE *author*

KRYSTLE A. BARRINGTON is an author, writer, and creative from Houston, Texas. Her passion is to encourage women to lean towards Christ and to live a life of joy through her writing. A cheerleader for self-love and overcoming past hurts, Krystle finds strength in speaking to women about her own personal struggles with learning to be comfortable in her own skin. She is also the author of *She Believes: 75 Devotionals to Encourage, Motivate, and Inspire*, available on Amazon.

For more about Krystle, please visit her online.
www.authorkrystlebarrington.com

www.ingramcontent.com/pod-product-compliance
Lightning Source LLC
Chambersburg PA
CBHW070854050426
42453CB00012B/2198